THE
VIVID
COLORS
OF THE
WOUNDS
OF
WAR

THE
VIVID
COLORS
OF THE
WOUNDS
OF
WAR

A COMBAT SOLDIER'S
PERSPECTIVE ON FREEDOM

DR. MIKE DUFFY

HHC, 1/505, 3/82D ABN DIV, USARV
SPEC 5 - HONORABLY DISCHARGED 4/DEC/1969

ISBN 979-8-9894314-0-3 (paperback)

All Scripture is taken from the AUTHORIZED KING JAMES VERSION.

Editing by Gretchen Doolittle
Cover design and typesetting by Jenneth Dyck

TABLE OF CONTENTS

INTRODUCTION

NOW, AS AN OLD MAN, I regularly find myself looking back over my life experience. My thoughts of a time that happened more than a half century ago, my tour in Vietnam, seem to return with greater frequency. It may be the lingering wounds and health issues of today that keep stirring the pot of remembrance of the seven and a half months of life-altering service in the steamy jungles, groves, and muddy country sides of the distant battlefield. Or it could be that my understanding of that time is coming more clearly into focus now with the wisdom of age and maturity. Or is it that I am being better informed by observing the world around me? You know, "there is nothing new under the sun!"

Today, my vision of politics and the affairs of

the world hold a greater interest for me as I understand their significance and relevance to the state of our Union. Things I once held dear and were priorities have diminished in importance and have faded into the background of time and reality. New things have taken their place.

While meditating on old memories recently, my thoughts turned to the idea of colors and how they relate to the wounds of war. These colors seemed to me to clarify the experiences I had during those challenging times. I started to think that these thoughts might be of interest to others and even encourage them or help others close the book on some horrible chapters of life they had to endure. And so, I thought recording them for posterity by authoring this little book seemed to be a good course of action. These colors are red, gold, purple, orange, and the invisible or colorless.

MY TOUR OF DUTY

DURING MY TOUR OF DUTY in Vietnam, our unit engaged in warfare out of forward fire-bases in "The Pineapple Region," located in the Mekong River delta, and "The Iron Triangle" near the Cambodian border. What my fellow soldiers and I experienced there was not conflict, it was WAR! Only in the minds of the heartless, cowardly politicians who feared using the word "war"—and refused to formally declare it war—would call it "a conflict." That was shameful! Gutless, pitiful leadership, for sure!

I was originally ordered to report to Company D of the 1/505th Infantry. However, immediately upon my arrival at our base camp compound along the runways of the Tan Son Nhut Air Base near Saigon, I was reassigned to Headquarters

Company and assigned the duty of driving the jeep for our battalion's S-1 officer. While the ride was great, the realities took me to the edge of fright on more than one occasion. A couple of months into this assignment, the captain rotated back to the States, and I was made our battalion's casualty clerk. Another soldier would be assigned to drive for the new S-1 officer.

Our entire brigade of the 82nd was withdrawn as a unit in early December 1969 as President Richard Nixon began to end America's participation in the war. I returned home and was honorably discharged on December 4, 1969. Our outfit (or military unit) was among the first troops to return to the States.

The Forward Firebase

Me and My Wheels!

RED:
THE RED CURRENCY
OF FREEDOM

TIME WILL NEVER DIM THE memory of my first day as a member of the 82nd. As the other new reinforcements and I jumped out of the truck that brought us from the in-country orientation to our bivouac area, I saw a body bag in use for the first time. The bag contained the lifeless body of a soldier who had been killed in a firefight just a couple hours earlier. It was a chilling sight to behold!

As two men lifted the bag and carefully placed it into the back of a jeep, I watched as "the red currency of freedom" poured from the bag on to the sandy soil, staining the ground of that foreign land. It was all the young second lieutenant had to offer. His life was over, his blood was shed, and a detachment of soldiers was already on their way to notify his young wife. Soon, his body would be returned to the States in a flag-draped coffin, but his blood would forever remain on the battlefield of freedom.

A stunning reality set into my life that day. Freedom isn't free! Far from it! Those of us who are living in freedom today should honor and express gratitude for those who have fought and died to obtain and preserve this precious gift. It was purchased at great cost.

His life was not the only one given. According to the National Archives, "The Vietnam Conflict Extract Data File of the Defense Casualty Analysis System (DCAS) Extract Files contains records of 58,220 U.S. military fatal casualties of the Vietnam War. These records were transferred into the custody of the National Archives and Records Administration in 2008. The earliest casualty record contains a date of death of June 8, 1956, and the most recent casualty record contains a date of death of May 28, 2006."[1] Imagine that! A half century of war and death!

Our maker commanded us to love one another as he has loved us, and this love is demonstrated through giving. Sometimes it was by giving everything, even their lives, to benefit others. Jesus Christ said to his disciples, "This is my commandment, That ye love one another, as I have loved you. Greater love hath no man than this, that a man lay down his life for his friends" (John 15:12–13). God gave his Son to pay the ultimate price, shedding his own blood, the red currency of freedom, so that we could be set free from the penalty and power of the sin that wars against our souls.

1 National Archive, "Vietnam War U.S. Military Fatal Casualty Statistics," Military Records, last reviewed August 23, 2022, https://www.archives.gov/research/military/vietnam-war/casualty-statistics#:~:text=April%2029%2C%202008.-,The%20 Vietnam%20Conflict%20Extract%20Data%20File%20of%20 the%20Defense%20Casualty,and%20Records%20Administration%20in%202008.

GOLD:
GOLD STAR FAMILIES

ALTHOUGH WE CAN NO LONGER voice our gratitude directly to our fallen heroes, we must understand that those who pay the ultimate sacrifice often leave behind a "gold star family." When one of my high school classmates was killed in action in Vietnam, his family became a gold star family. At the time, it seemed awkward to be with them because it seemed as if words would do little to mitigate the grief they were experiencing. The sense of sadness and helplessness was influential.

According to the U.S. Army's website, "The term Gold Star Family is a modern reference that comes from the Service Flag. . . . The flag included a blue star for every immediate family member serving in the armed forces of the United States, during any period of war or hostilities in which the armed forces of the United States were engaged. If that loved one died, the blue star was replaced by a gold star. This allowed members of the community to know the price that the family had paid in the cause of freedom. . . . The strength of our nation is our Army. The strength of our Army is our Soldiers. The strength of our Soldiers is our families. The Army recognizes that no one has given more for the nation than the families of the fallen."[1]

I don't remember these banners or flags being used during the Vietnam War. Perhaps it was the controversial nature and national rejection of the war that created a stigma or shame that prevented families of service members from using them. My experience of returning from the war would be consistent with this probability.

As a father and now a grandfather and great-grandfather, I cannot begin to comprehend the pain and suffering these gold star wives, parents, and families must endure for a lifetime. Do you know any? How is it that you reach out and help them? True gratitude requires action!

---

1 U.S. Army, "Gold Star Survivors," U.S. Army, accessed September 29, 2023, https://www.army.mil/goldstar/.

World War II-era Service Flag

PURPLE:
THE PURPLE HEART

THE PURPLE HEART IS A medal presented in the name of the sitting president to service members who have been wounded or killed as a result of enemy action while serving in the United States military. A Purple Heart is a solemn tribute indicating a service member has made a great personal sacrifice while in the line of duty.

While serving our country in Vietnam as the casualty clerk for our battalion, it was my job to communicate with the medivac helicopters and field hospitals to get a prognosis on each member of our outfit who had been wounded. In the course of gathering this information so next of kin could be properly notified, I would record

The Purple Heart

the circumstances surrounding the action and identify where the wound or injury occurred. Armed with that knowledge, I would then draft the narrative that would accompany the letter of condolence or the award of The Purple Heart medal.

Before I had ever stepped foot on Vietnamese soil, a high school classmate and close friend of mine was awarded The Purple Heart posthumously. His name was John W. Vowels, better known to us as "Jack." We graduated together from Hiawatha High School in Kirkland, Illinois, on June 6, 1966. His family farmed near the little village of Irene, a few miles northwest of Kirkland. Less than two months after his twenty-first birthday, on January 21, 1969, Jack made the ultimate sacrifice for America as a forward artillery observer in the Marine Corps. His earthly battles were over, and he moved on to his eternal dwelling place! His family had a new designation, "Gold Star Family."

If you know a Purple Heart recipient or a gold star family, as you have opportunity, reach out and thank them. August 7 is National Purple Heart Day in America, and the last Sunday in September is the day to honor gold star families. Perhaps a phone call or a card expressing remembrance and gratitude will be a help. A post on social media may also be meaningful to those who have been wounded or killed while protecting our nation.

ORANGE: AGENT ORANGE

IT TOOK DECADES BEFORE THE major effects of exposure to the chemical defoliant "Agent Orange" showed up on my body, but it did show up. My study of this chemical indicated that its use was at its peak when I was in Vietnam, and our unit was in one of the heaviest areas of concentration in which it was used, the Iron Triangle, a hostile area not too far from the Cambodian border.

It first showed up on me as skin cancer, then chemically induced neuropathy in my legs, attacking the nerve conductivity below both my knees. Eventually, the exposure resulted in no nerve activity whatsoever below either knee. My

25

lower legs and feet had no feeling whatsoever. Today, I have to look down to see where my feet actually are to know that they are there! No feeling at all. They are paralyzed to a degree.

This condition was diagnosed as "chemically induced neuropathy" and has had a tremendous negative impact on my balance. I lost my ability to walk around without the aid of a cane or a walker. I could no longer enjoy the activities of life that I had once enjoyed—golfing, fishing trips, and sporting activities. I became a "high risk for falling." Just in the past year, I have had three falls that resulted in broken bones. Eventually, the Veterans Administration determined me to be 100 percent disabled because of it. Even today, they are discovering more long-term effects and recognizing them as "presumptive," since the conditions were common and identical for so many who served in that theatre.

I have to admit that it makes me wonder about some of the other health issues I have faced through life, including the joint replacement of both knees and one hip, the decrease density of my bones as they continue deteriorating and thinning, and the major resection of my small and large intestines that doctors said had "unusual symptoms and damage" and was "quite severe." The surgeon that opened me up for that surgery said to my wife and two daughters who were standing by, "This is a very sick man!" I can only say "By God's grace, I made it through the surgery and lengthy recovery process."

The wounds of this kind of "friendly fire," as unintentional as they may have been, have damaged the body, soul, and spirit of an untold number of veterans. Tens of thousands of my fellow Vietnam vets have died of cancers resulting from exposure to this deadly chemical. The irony here is mind boggling! The use of Agent Orange in Vietnam was intended to save the lives of those that it has since killed after returning home! Go figure! I have had VA appointments with the dermatology department every four to six months for the past dozen years. Each time I go, they burn, freeze, or cut several cancerous spots off my body! The wounds just keep coming!

Agent Orange has also radically altered the course of life for an untold number of others. Debilitation caused by this chemical has cost veterans the loss of senses including touch, hearing, sight, smell, and taste. It is the source of chronic illness, terminal illness, and disability that have become commonplace among these aging warriors. How do you categorize these wounds?

What do you call this kind of damage? It seems far too convenient and easy to brush it off as the "collateral damage of war" without considering they are wounds, serious wounds, life-altering wounds, to our soldiers.

Although there were no medals given for these injuries, I am grateful that these issues have been identified and continue to be discovered and recognized by the VA. It demonstrates to me that the country has begun caring for us. For decades, it seemed to me they did not care, rather, they were ashamed of us. There is so much more that needs to be done, and the clock is ticking!

Aerial herbicide spray missions in southern Viet Nam, 1965 to 1971 (Source: U.S. Dept. of the Army).

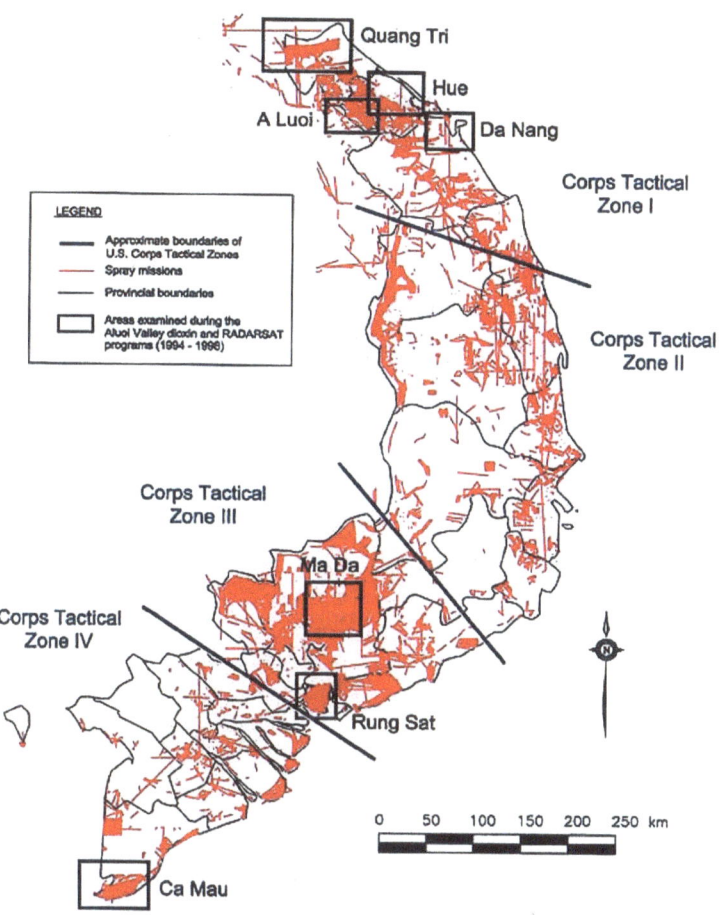

INVISIBLE OR COLORLESS: PTSD AND SUICIDE

ALTHOUGH INVISIBLE OR COLORLESS are considered to be "colors" in this story, we do seem to recognize them to be an oxymoron. "A colorless color?" However, it is an accurate representation of real battlefield wounds. Sometimes things that are, cannot easily be seen. Instead, they appear "colorless."

PTSD

My invisible wounds were identified by my doctors, therapists, and group leaders as "mental" wounds and "moral" wounds. I have been officially diagnosed with Post Traumatic Stress Dis-

order (PTSD), resulting in extreme claustropho-
bia and the accompanying anxiety.

As I looked back on my service, that diagno-
sis was no surprise to me. The "tunnel rats" in
our unit had many casualties, including bullet
wounds, concussions, and various other wounds
from cleverly placed booby traps. I document-
ed the circumstances of these instances and got
the prognosis from those who were treating their
wounds. It was through the work of these brave
soldiers that the 82nd uncovered weapons caches
and enemy hideouts. In fact, we located the larg-
est underground complex ever discovered during
the entire Vietnam War. Documenting the cir-
cumstantial details of these casualties is indelibly
etched on my mind—an invisible wound.

Trauma is often described as "an emotional
response that is trapped." It cannot express or ex-
haust itself to properly, or adequately, address the
issue or event that triggered it. It short-circuits
and stresses a person's "intellect-feeling-decision"
process, leaving the emotional response trapped
inside and the person "stuck." A leading profes-
sional trauma therapist once explained trauma to
me like this:

> Trauma occurs when an event or experi-
> ence overwhelms our mind or body to the

degree that we cannot respond in the usu-
al fight-or-flight capacity. In this instance,
our mind and body completely shut down,
ceasing to function to their ability, until the
actual or perceived danger has passed. Two
things occur when the mind and body shut
down. First, the event or experience is not
processed through the cortex part of our
brain (the thinking, logical part), but it remains trapped in the limbic part of our
brain (the part that is based on emotions,
has no concept of time, and remains un-
processed). Secondly, what takes place is
that all our survival responses get trapped
in our body and are unable to be cycled out
through our natural fight-or-flight cycle.
When we are in fear, the body (central ner-
vous system) is rushed with stress hormones
to get us ready for fight or flight. If that
natural cycle is stopped due to dissociation,
those bodily responses stay activated in our
body. These survival responses such as rapid
heart and respiratory rate, increased blood
pressure, sweating, changes in our intestinal
tract, nausea, anxiousness, to name a few,
become so overwhelming day after day that
individuals will do anything to get rid of

the hypervigilance, impending doom, and chronic fear. This is where our unhealthy coping mechanisms and addictions come into play. Once the body finds something that will relieve the chronic fear and activation, the mind will do anything to replicate that and go after it at all costs.

Deployment alone was certainly traumatic, and in many ways, life changing. As I left home to report for duty in Vietnam, I left behind my wife of just a year and a half and our first son, born a few days before my departure. That was traumatic. Exposure to the blood and the bodies day after day in Vietnam often triggered the "fight-or-flight response" of my emotions. That was quite traumatic! Getting the news from a field hospital and then writing about it, and doing this for days, weeks, and months upon end was traumatic. I grew up more in those eight months than at any other time in my life. I often say, even today, I would not trade the experience for anything, but I would not want to go through it again!

Medals and Memories — Tokens of Trauma

SUICIDE

There is another "invisible wound." Suicide! If you stop and give some serious thought to this issue, you soon realize that hopelessness is often the precursor to suicide. It is the last step before the act. When all hope is gone, and the pain is too great to bear, in the minds of some, suicide offers a quick and easy way out! Out to where? That may be the most important question.

The National Library of Medicine has estimated more than 50,000 Vietnam Veterans have committed suicide![1] There seems to be conflicting numbers as I found out in my own research. Some say as many as 100,000 committed suicide following the end of the Vietnam War.[2] Whatever the number is, why? Why so many suicides? While the vicious day-after-day exposure to the violence and the blood and guts of war would certainly contribute to this, some just cannot escape the horrors in their minds. The sounds and scenes show up every night in dreams referred to as "night terrors." I guess time doesn't heal all wounds! Even with the pain-killing balm of drugs or alcohol, some just cannot continue coping. Those mind and mood-altering substances are not enough!

---

1 D. A. Pollock, P. Rhodes, C. A. Boyle, P. Decoufle, and D. L. McGee, "Estimating the Number of Suicides among Vietnam Veterans," *American Journal of Psychiatry* 147, no. 6 (June 1990): 772–776, https://pubmed.ncbi.nlm.nih.gov/2343923/.

2 The New York Times, "How Many Suicides by Vietnam Veterans," Opinion, The New York Times, published March 7, 1991, https://web.archive.org/web/20130205174239/https://www.nytimes.com/1991/03/07/opinion/l-how-many-suicides-by-vietnam-vets-841091.html.

And, then the experience of coming home and being rejected by the nation that ordered you to the battlefield was just too much to take. No semblance of fairness there! It did not take us long to experience this cruel, thoughtless behavior. For me, within an hour of being discharged and walking out the gates of the Oakland Army Depot, dressed in newly issued khakis that replaced the filthy and tattered jungle attire I wore on the flight back to the States and donned with the medals of service, I was hurled with the hateful psychological bombs. As my two combat buddies and I made our way to the airport in San Francisco for our flights home, the jeers and the heartless words, accompanied with disgusting sneers and hostile gestures, became more frequent.

Rejection and shame are powerful weapons that can destroy a person, especially when they seem to keep coming at you. Eventually, the haunting overtakes the rational soul. After enduring so much of the rejection, many Vietnam vets responded by closing down or shutting people out. We were tired of the pain and agony of war. To also face a steady diet of this hatred and rejection was not tolerable! How long would we remain psychological prisoners of war?

My cousin, Eddie Duffy, worked less than two hundred yards from my post in our rear area located in Phu Loi, South Vietnam. He was a supply specialist for the 1/508 BN, 3/82D ABN DIV, US-ARV. We often thought of how amazing this coincidence was. Imagine the chances of cousins who grew up in nearby small towns in northern Illinois, with populations of less than a thousand, serving their country halfway around the world and then being stationed this close together. As crazy as this was, it certainly provided moments of comfort and reflection. The comfort was especially important as we endured the cesspool of war.

When President Nixon ordered the 82nd to return to the States, any of us who had fewer than five months remaining on our tour of duty were rotated back to the States, and many of that group were discharged at that time. Anyone with more than five months remaining on their tour was reassigned to another unit in-country. Eddie was just outside the window of those who would rotate home. He was reassigned to an infantry battalion of the 101st Airborne which was located at that time in a very hostile area known as A Shau Valley.

While stationed in Phu Loi, there were occasions where Eddie and I spent time together, and we would often talk of home and family. Eddie was the second oldest of ten kids in their family. He loved children. It seemed as though whenever we enjoyed this time together, the conversation would eventually come around to the suffering we witnessed in the lives of the little children in Vietnam. It was awful, and it was abundant! For anyone with a compassionate heart, it was difficult to observe, especially having no avenue or platform to help them.

Although we do not know all the details, after Eddie was reassigned to the 101st, the suffering and pain of the war became too great. He turned to drug use to ease that pain. With all kinds of exotics available, and easy to acquire, many soldiers tried to mask their hurt by seeking and using them. Unfortunately, Eddie was no exception. In his case, the drugs fried his brain.

When Eddie eventually got home, he sought help at Hines Veterans Hospital near Chicago. Although experiencing some initial treatment success, the damage was so great that hopelessness set in, and Eddie committed suicide. Through his colorless wounds, Eddie became an invisible casualty of war! He's not even mentioned on the Illinois

Vietnam War Casualties list.[3] What a travesty! How sad! Eddie's sacrifice is memorialized on a small parcel of land in a quiet little cemetery just outside the village of Lee! Eddie has since been recognized on the Vietnam Veterans Memorial Fund website.[4] Thank you, Eddie, rest in peace!

Eddie's Final Resting Place

---

3 Kim Torp, "Illinois Vietnam War Casualties," Military Genealogy Trails, updated in 2006, http://genealogytrails.com/ill/vietnamcas2.html#d.

4 Vietnam Veterans Memorial Fund, "Edward Duffy," In Memory Honor Roll, posted on September 15, 2011, https://www.vvmf.org/Honor-Roll/479/EdwardJamesDuffy/.

HONOR TO WHOM HONOR IS DUE

HAVE YOU EVER NOTICED HOW the passing of time quickly diminishes the honoring of those who deserve the recognition? This is why we need reminders. The Apostle Paul exhorted the believers at the church in Rome, "Render therefore to all their dues: tribute to whom tribute is due; custom to whom custom; fear to whom fear; honour to whom honour" Romans 13:7.

Thomas Jefferson, the third President of the United States, said, "My God! How little do my countrymen know what precious blessings they are in possession of, and which no other people on earth enjoy."[1] He served two terms as our nation's leader. Jefferson knew that it was through the service of brave men that the other countrymen could "know what precious blessing" it was to live in the greatest country on earth.

From a grateful veteran to all who have served our nation in the cause of freedom, this book is dedicated to you. And so, I stand and salute you—I honor you with these published memories. From the deepest recesses of my heart, I say:

THANK YOU! THANK YOU! THANK YOU!

And may God's blessing be on you and yours, for both now and eternity. And here is a special message from my heart, with love, to my fellow Vietnam veterans:

WELCOME HOME!

You are a winner!

You are an American patriot!

We are SOLDIERS!

---

1 Thomas Jefferson, "From Thomas Jefferson to James Monroe, 17 June 1785," Founders Online, National Archives, accessed September 29, 2023, https://founders.archives.gov/documents/Jefferson/01-08-02-0174.

LEST WE FORGET

SO MANY CITIZENS FROM EVERY generation of our great nation have suffered from the wounds of war. The fight for freedom seems to never end. While peace for all is desirable, the reality is that the enemy of freedom and peace is always on the attack. We must stand and fight! And because we must, some will pay a heavy price. We are grateful for all who stand in harms way, willing to sacrifice to defend our precious freedom. We must never forget them. NEVER!

Of the 2.7 million men and women who served in the Vietnam War, 58,220 paid the ultimate sacrifice.[1] However, there are 58,318 names memorialized on "The Wall" in Washington D.C., as of 2017.[2]

---

1 National Archive, "Vietnam War U.S. Military."

2 Vietnam Veterans Memorial Fund, "Vietnam Veterans Memorial: The Names," accessed September 29, 2023, https://www.vvmf.org/About-The-Wall/the-names/.

THE VIETNAM VETERANS MEMORIAL
"These names, seemingly infinite in number . . ."

It's the most-visited memorial on the National Mall in Washington, attracting more than 5 million people each year—the Vietnam Veterans Memorial. The most prominent feature of the memorial is a massive wall that lists the names. . . .
"The Vietnam Veterans Memorial wall was dedicated on Veterans Day in 1982, fulfilling one veteran's promise to never forget those who served and sacrificed during the Vietnam War. [3]

------

3 U.S. Department of Defense, "Vietnam Veterans Memorial," accessed September 29, 2023, https://www.defense.gov/Multimedia/Experience/Vietnam-Veterans-Memorial/.

When they announced the building of the wall, I thought, "It is about time." Looking back on that thought now makes me think that may have been the beginning of a healing process that has been happening for decades. Why has it taken so long to heal? Occasionally, the proverbial scab gets picked off the wounds and the healing process starts again. The encounter with or the sight of a homeless vet, or the casual use of the word "conflict" when referring to the war seem to trigger in me the memories and raw emotion from one of the most impactful experiences of my life.

I remember the first time I visited the memorial and will never forget the irony of walking up to the wall and one of the first names I saw was the sergeant with whom I had served and for whom I cataloged the circumstance and details surrounding his death on the battlefield. It was a strange moment that conjured up a fountain of tears and brought to mind, with amazing clarity, some of what we all experienced in the beauty and ugliness of Vietnam.

I had a teacher in college who began most class sessions by saying: "If there is one thing we fail to learn from history, it is that we fail to learn from history." When this happens, we are doomed to repeat history, even the "bad stuff!"

The Pledge of Allegiance to the Flag should serve as a constant reminder of the value of remembering. When I was a child, we recited the pledge every morning at school at the beginning of the day. We are failing our children today by not furthering this practice. Many have abandoned the practice because they do not want to "offend" students who would not be willing to make the pledge. How shameful! Where is our godly leadership and spirit of patriotism? Just because a few people do not want to embrace the identity of America, we Americans should not be asked to neuter ourselves of this identity. That is just foolishness! This IS America!

"I pledge allegiance to the flag of the United States of America, and to the republic for which it stands, one nation under God, indivisible, with liberty and justice for all."

As our founding fathers were establishing this country, even they recognized the importance of remembering the history of the land. I have come to realize how easy it is for a nation to forget about the cost of freedom. The cost of war and the lessons we learn from them quickly fade into the archives of history because of the busyness and opportunities each of us relish in the present. We need the occasional reminder to bring reality to the value we should place on freedom.

And as passive as that thought may seem, we must understand also that the enemies of freedom are constantly trying to rewrite history or at least cause us to minimize its importance.

Great leaders in our nation's past have emphasized the need to remember. Many of them have reminded us of the importance of the Bible's influence on our founding and history. They have attributed the greatness of our past to the embracing of the truth of the Bible.

A nation which does not remember what it was yesterday, does not know what it is today, nor what it is trying to do. We are trying to do a futile thing if we do not know where we came from or what we have been about. —Woodrow Wilson[4]

America's quest for freedom and liberty has its roots in the Bible.

When the Reformation swept over Europe, it put the Bible in the hands of the people,

4 Woodrow Wilson, "Robert E. Lee: An Interpretation," *Social Forces* 2, no. 3 (March 1924): 321–328, https://doi. org/10.2307/3006289. Also available for full viewing at: https://leefamilyarchive.org/reference/essays/wilson/index. html#:~:text=Now%20the%20same%20is%20true,what%20 we%20have%20been%20about.

revolutionized concepts of government and set the stage for the American Republic. With the influence of Samuel Rutherford, John Witherspoon and John Locke, the Bible became the basis of United States government and law. —John W. Whitehead[5]

Not only does our nation find its foundational principles of government in Scripture, but its laws are designed to shape a culture of righteousness and peace. Consider the following from one of America's great patriots:

The moral principles and precepts contained in the Scriptures ought to form the basis of all our civil constitutions and laws. . . . All the miseries and evils which men suffer from vice, crime, ambition, injustice, oppression, slavery, and war, proceed from their despising or neglecting the precepts contained in the Bible. —Noah Webster[6]

---

5 Nancy Leigh Demoss, ed., *The Rebirth of America* (West Palm Beach, FL: Arthur S. DeMoss Foundation, 1986), 35.

6 Dr. Alan Snyder, "Great Quotes by: Noah Webster," Pondering Principles, accessed September 29, 2023, https://ponderingprinciples.com/quotes/webster/.

George Washington, in his initial inaugural address to Congress, said:

> No People can be bound to acknowledge and adore the invisible hand, which conducts the Affairs of men more than the People of the United States. Every step, by which they have advanced to the character of an independent nation, seems to have been distinguished by some token of providential agency. . . . We ought to be no less persuaded that the propitious smiles of Heaven can never be expected on a nation that disregards the eternal rules of order and right, which Heaven itself has ordained.[7]

Our nation's first president realized that the American experiment was the design and plan of Almighty God, and if it were to survive and thrive, the authority and ways of God must be foremost in the hearts and minds of her people.

Abraham Lincoln said:

> All the good the Saviour [*sic*] gave to the world was communicated through this

---

7 George Washington, "Washington's Inaugural Address of 1789," American Originals, National Archives and Records Administration, accessed September 29, 2023, https://www.archives.gov/exhibits/american_originals/inaugtxt.html.

book. But for it we could not know right from wrong. All things most desirable for man's welfare . . . are to be found portrayed in it.[8]

Lincoln's understanding and resolve was rooted in God's Holy Word. It led him through one of the most difficult times in American history, the Civil War.

---

8 Abraham Lincoln, "Collected Works of Abraham Lincoln," vol. 7, accessed September 29, 2023, https://quod.lib.umich. edu/cgi/t/text/text-idx?c=lincoln;rgn=div1;view=text;id-no=lincoln7;node=lincoln7:1184.

FREEDOM IS NOT FREE, IT COMES AT A GREAT PRICE

Posterity! You will never know, how much it has cost the present Generation, to preserve your Freedom! I hope you will make good Use of it. —John Adams[1]

THE DRAFTERS AND SIGNERS OF the Declaration of Independence were committed to freedom when they included the following in the text: "For the support of this Declaration, with

---

1 John Adams, "John Adams to Abigail Adams, 26 April 1777," Founders Online, National Archives, accessed September 29, 2023, https://founders.archives.gov/documents/Adams/04-02-02-0169#:~:text=Posterity!,the%20Pains%20to%20preserve%20it.

a firm reliance on the protection of the divine Providence, we mutually pledge to each other our Lives, our Fortunes, and our sacred Honor."[2] They knew, and understood, there was a price to pay, and they were willing to pay it!

The Apostle Paul, writing to the church in Galatia, said, "Stand fast therefore in the liberty wherewith Christ hath made us free, and be not entangled again with the yoke of bondage" Galatians 5:1.

I took Jesus at his Word on January 21, 1980, and asked him to forgive me and save me from the penalty and power of my sin. He did! He healed me! He changed me! HE SET ME FREE! He provided the red currency of freedom—his blood—to pay a debt I owed that was so great that I could not pay it. I needed a Savior! And because of his great love for me, he laid down his life, took upon himself my sin burden and its penalty, and died on a cruel cross! For the hurting and wounded, healing begins with a person, Jesus Christ!

---

2 Thomas Jefferson, et al., Declaration of Independence, Philadelphia, PA, July 4, 1776. Can also be accessed at: https://www.archives.gov/founding-docs/declaration-transcript.

Come unto me, all ye that labour and are heavy laden, and I will give you rest. Take my yoke upon you, and learn of me; for I am meek and lowly in heart: and ye shall find rest unto your souls. For my yoke is easy, and my burden is light. (Matthew 11:28–30)

Jesus Christ gave this invitation to the universe, and he is still waiting for you to accept it.

THE LAST BEST HOPE ON EARTH

IT IS SHAMEFUL FOR A country to allow their combat veterans—those who have left the safety and comfort of home and the presence of their loved ones for extended periods of time—to experience constant peril in fighting and dying to preserve liberty and freedom and then to struggle, suffer, and die as the freedom-loving citizenry walks by or steps over them. Far too many are cast to the gutter or the ditches of life unattended to. People look at them as though their alcoholism and addiction have caused their awful condition. Really? Are they the cause? Or are they the symptoms of the real cause? Someone better get an answer to that question soon. Every day that passes is "too late" for many. Those who revel in the benefits of freedom are tasked with electing representatives to serve in government. It is these civil servants who have the power to make changes that will honorably care for the veteran. Unfortunately, the quest for political power and personal greed is a powerful force that undermine the priority list of care for the veteran. I know! And it hurts! Wake up America! Wake up! We are crying out to you to WAKE UP AND HELP!

According to the Constitution that binds our nation into a perfect union, "providing for the common defense" is the primary responsibility of the government. All the other responsibilities seem to fall under the "promoting the general welfare." Is "providing" limited to arming us and then sending us to the battlefield? What if we do not come back whole? What if we do not come back to our families at all? What are our wives and children to do? Their protector and provider was engaged by their country to provide for this common defense, and now, they have given their one life for the country, our country! It was to "secure the blessings of liberty" for us! Can we just walk away now? Will we?

As our free nation teeters on the brink of extinction, as a people, we face together a crisis of historical magnitude, and we need a new generation of patriots with the courage and resolve to stand up and shout from the rooftops of America, "*Never Again!*" To quote President Ronald Reagan as he addressed the nation at his inauguration, he declared that "freedom is a fragile thing and it's never more than one generation away from extinction."[1]

Red, Gold, Purple, Orange, And Invisible!

THE VIVID COLORS OF THE WOUNDS OF WAR!

---

1 Ronald Reagan, "January 5, 1967: Inaugural Address (Public Ceremony)," Archives, Ronald Reagan Presidential Library and Museum, accessed October 7, 2023, https://www.reaganlibrary.gov/archives/speech/january-5-1967-inaugural-address-public-ceremony.

ABOUT THE AUTHOR

DR. MIKE DUFFY AND HIS wife of fifty-six years have three children together, twelve grand-children, and four great-grandchildren. Mike's life experience is characterized by service, integrity, leadership, and accomplishment. He grew up in a home that was shattered by alcoholism when he was in elementary school. Overcoming this tragedy and trauma early in life, he has experienced productivity and success on many levels.

Mike is a combat veteran who served a tour in Vietnam with an infantry battalion of the United States Army's Eighty-Second Airborne Division. He learned early the value and reward of working hard and excelled in a corporate career for fourteen years in administrative management and sales, receiving international awards at each level for outstanding achievement and accomplishment.

Mike received Jesus Christ as his personal Savior at age thirty-one and committed his life to Christian ministry at age thirty-five, ministering God's Word in nearly one thousand ministries nationally and internationally.

He has authored other books based on his life experience including, *The Tragedies and Triumphs in an Alcoholic's Family* and *Grandpa Saw the Light*.

The following statement from Mike reveals his heart: "There is trauma and tragedy everywhere. I believe that everyone will face some adversity in life. How one responds to that adversity will shape their future. People can be paralyzed, damaged, or destroyed when adversity comes, or they can use adversity as motivation for positive change. We cannot change the past, but we do not have to live there either. We must learn from the past, look toward the future, but live today. Although no one can go back and change their beginning, they can begin today to change their ending. This is what hope looks like. I love serving God and others and have found that this approach in life is the pathway to happiness.

www.ingramcontent.com/pod-product-compliance
Lightning Source LLC
Chambersburg PA
CBHW040857120626
46551CB00001B/65